Horace Walpole, Paul Hentzner

A Journey into England in the Year MDXCVIII

Horace Walpole, Paul Hentzner

A Journey into England in the Year MDXCVIII

ISBN/EAN: 9783744798464

Printed in Europe, USA, Canada, Australia, Japan

Cover: Foto ©Andreas Hilbeck / pixelio.de

More available books at **www.hansebooks.com**

A Journey into England

In the Year Mdxcviii.

BY

PAUL HENTZNER

Being a Translation of Part of His Itinerary.

EDITED BY

HORACE WALPOLE.

~~~~~~~~

"Don, O Books, are the golden bessels of the Temple; burning lamps to be eber held in the hand."

RICHARD AUNGERVYLE.

~~~~~~~~

PRIVATELY PRINTED FOR THE AUNGERVYLE SOCIETY,

EDINBURGH.

1881.

INTRODUCTION.

PAUL HENTZNER'S "Itinerarium Germaniae, Galliae, Angliae, et Italiae," was first published at Nuremberg in 1612. It is a small 4to, and is of the greatest rarity in England: that it was so even in the middle of the last century, is proved by Horace Walpole's statement in his Advertisement, that there were only four or five copies then in this country. A copy in the Stevens' sale sold for £3, 10s It was reprinted at Breslau in 1617, 4to; and Nuremberg in 1618 and 1629, both 8vo—the latter edition being considerably augmented, though not by any means improved. A copy of the 1629 edition appears in the Hibbert Catalogue: it sold for £3, 1s. The last edition was that of Leipzig, 1661, 8vo.

Struck with the picture which it presented of the Court of Queen Elizabeth, Horace Walpole employed Richard Bentley, son of the doctor, to translate that part which relates to England. Only two hundred and twenty copies of this translation were printed at Strawberry Hill in 1757, 8vo, and it is consequently but rarely that a copy occurs for sale, and then it invariably fetches a high price, even when it does not happen to contain so important an autograph as that of David Garrick, at whose sale, in 1779, it brought £2, 3s.—a large price for a book in those days, when Dibdin had not yet turned the bibliophiles of England into so many biblio-maniacs.

In 1797, Jeffrey published an 8vo edition of Bentley's trans-lation, with portraits and views, supplemented with Sir Robert Naunton's Fragmenta Regalia, which, though very inaccurate, soon became scarce and dear.

Ten years later, in 1807, T. E. Williams printed, at his private press, an edition of fifty copies, 4to.

The author of the Itinerarium, Paul Hentzner, was tutor to a young German nobleman, and, with his pupil, visited Germany, England, France, and Italy. The circumstances and customs which the author records will be found interest-ing to the English antiquarian, whilst even the historian may find some crumbs of information worthy of being picked up.

"The author seems to have had that laborious and indis-criminate passion for *seeing* which is remarked in his country-men; and, as his translator observed, enjoyed as much the doubtful head of a more doubtful saint in pickle, as any upon the shoulders of the best Grecian statue. Fortunately, so memorable a personage as Queen Elizabeth happened to fall under his notice. Ten years later, he would have been as accurate in painting Anne of Denmark!"

28

With the above quotation from Horace Walpole's Advertisement to his edition, we close our Introduction, merely observing that if we have passed over the remainder of the Advertisement in silence, it is because readers in these days would care little for ill-natured remarks on Monsieur de Bassompierre's orthography of English names, with which the Earl of Orford thought fit to preface Hentzner's really curious and striking narration.

E. M. G.

W. F. F.

HENTZNER'S TRAVELS.

———•———

E arrived at RYE, a small *English* Seaport. Here, as soon as we came on shore, we gave in our names to the Notary of the place, but not till he had demanded our business; and being answered, that we had none but to see *England*, we were conducted to an inn, where we were very well entertained, as one generally is in this country.

We took post horses for *London*. It is surprising how swiftly they run, their bridles are very light, and their saddles, little more than a span over.

FLIMWELL, a village; here we returned our first horses, and mounted fresh ones.

We passed through TUNBRIDGE, another village.

CHEPSTED, another village; here for a second time we changed horses.

LONDON, the head and metropolis of *England;* called by *Tacitus,* LONDINIUM; by *Ptolomey,* LONGIDINIUM; by *Ammianus Marcellinus,* LUNDINIUM; by foreigners, LONDRA and LONDRES; is the seat of the *British* Empire, and the chamber of the *English* kings. This most ancient City is in the county of *Middlesex,* the fruitfullest and wholsomest soil in England. It is built upon the River *Thames,*

60 miles from the sea, and was originally founded, as all historians agree, *by Brutus*, who coming from *Greece* into *Italy*, thence into *Africa*, next into *France*, and last into *Britain*, chose this situation, for the convenience of the river, calling it *Troja nova*, which name was afterwards corrupted into *Trinovant.* But when *Lud*, the brother of *Cassibilan* or *Cassevelan*, who wared against *Julius Caesar*, as he himself mentions, *lib.* v. *de Bell. Gall.* came to the crown, he encompassed it with very strong walls, and towers very artfully constructed, and from his own name called it *Caier Lud*, i.e. *Lud's* city. This name was corrupted into that of *Caerlunda*, and again in time, by change of language, into *Lundres.* *Lud*, when he died, was buried in this town, near that Gate which is yet called in *Welch*, *Por Lud*, in *Saxon*, *Ludesgate.*

The famous River THAMES owes part of its stream, as well as of its appellation, to the *Isis*, rising a little above *Winchelcomb*, and being increased with several rivulets, unites both its waters and its name to the *Thame*, on the other side of *Oxford;* thence after passing by *London*, and being of the utmost utility, from its greatness and navigation, it opens into a vast arm of the sea, from whence the tide, according to *Gemma Frissius*, flows and ebbs to the distance of 80 miles, twice in twenty-five hours, and according to *Polydore Virgil*, above 60 miles, twice in twenty-four hours.

This City being very large of itself, has very extensive Suburbs, and a Fort called the *Tower*, of beautiful structure. It is magnificently ornamented with public buildings and churches, of which there are above 120 Parochial. On the south is a Bridge of stone, 800 feet in length, of wonderful work; it is supported upon 20 Piers of square stone, 60 feet high, and 30 broad, joined by Arches of about 20 feet diameter. The whole is covered on each side with houses, so disposed as to have the appearance of a continued street, not at all of a bridge.

Upon this is built a Tower, on whose top the heads of such as have been executed for High Treason, are placed upon iron spikes. We counted above 30.

Paulus Jovius, in his description of the most remarkable Towns in *England*, says, all are obscured by *London*, which, in the opinion of many, is *Caesar's* city of the *Trinobantes*, the capital of all *Britain*, famous for the commerce of many nations; its houses are elegantly built, its churches fine, its towns strong, and its riches and abundance surprizing. The wealth of the world is wafted to it by the *Thames*, swelled by the tide and navigable to merchant's ships through a safe and deep channel for 60 miles from its mouth to the city. Its banks are everywhere beautified with fine country seats, woods, and farms; below, is the Royal Palace of *Greenwich*; above, that of Richmond; and between both, on the west of *London*, rise the noble buildings of *Westminster*, most remarkable for the Courts of Justice, the Parliament, and *St Peter's* Church, enriched with the Royal Tombs. At the distance of 20 miles from *London*, is the Castle of *Windsor*, a most delightful retreat of the Kings of *England*, as well as famous for several of their Tombs, and for the ceremonial of the Order of the Garter. This river abounds in swans, swimming in flocks; the sight of them and their noise is vastly agreeable to the Fleets that meet them in their course. It is joined to the City by a bridge of stone, wonderfully built; is never encreased by any rains, rising only with the tide, and is everywhere spread with nets for the taking of salmon and shad. Thus far Paulus Jovius.

Polydore Virgil affirms, that *London* has continued to be a royal city, and the capital of the kingdom, crowded with its own inhabitants and foreigners, abounding in riches, and famous for its great trade, from the time of King *Archeninus*, or *Erchenvinus*. Here the Kings are crowned, and solemnly inaugurated, and the Council of the nation or Parliament is held. The Government of the City is lodged by ancient grant of the Kings of *Britain*, in twenty-four Aldermen, that is seniors. These annually elect out of their own body a Mayor, and two Sheriffs, who determine causes according to municipal laws. It has always had, as indeed *Britain* in general, a great number of men of learning, much distinguished for their writings. The walls are pierced with six gates, which, as they were rebuilt, acquired new names. Two look eastward :

(1) LUDGATE, the oldest, so called from King *Lud*, whose name is yet to be seen, cut into the stone over the arch on one side ; though others imagine it rather to have been *Fludgate*, from a stream over which it stands, like the *Porta Fluentana* at *Rome*. It has been lately repaired by Queen *Elizabeth*, whose statue is placed on the opposite side ; and

(2) NEWGATE, the best edifice of any: so called from being newly built, whereas before it was named *Chamberlain Gate*. It is the public Prison.

On the north are four :

(1) ALDERSGATE, as some think, from Alder Trees ; as others, from *Aldricius*, a *Saxon*.

(2) CRIPLEGATE, from an Hospital for the lame.

(3) MOORGATE, from a neighbouring morass, now converted into a field, first opened by *Francetius the Mayor, A.D. 1414.

(4) And BISHOPSGATE, from some bishop. This the German merchants of the *Hans* Society were obliged by compact to keep in repair, and in times of danger to defend. They were in possession of a key, to open or shut it, so that upon occasion they could come in, or go out, by night or by day.

There is only one gate to the east :

ALDGATE, that is *Oldgate*, from its antiquity ; though others think it to have been named *Elbegate*.

Several people believe there were formerly two gates (besides that to the bridge) towards the *Thames*.

---

* His name was Sir Thomas Falconer.

(1) BILLINGSGATE, now a cothon, or artificial Port, for the reception of ships.

(2) DOURGATE, vulgo *Dowgate* i.e. *Water-gate*.

The CATHEDRAL OF ST PAUL was founded by *Ethelbert*, King of the *Saxons*, and being from time to time re-edified, encreased to vastness and magnificence, and in revenue so much, that it affords a plentiful support to a Bishop, Dean, Precentor, Treasurer, four Arch-Deacons, twenty-nine Prebendaries, and many others. The roof of this Church, as of most others in *England*, with the adjoining steeple, is covered with lead.

On the other side of the choir is the marble tomb of *Nicholas Bacon*, with his wife. Not far from this is a magnificent monument, ornamented with pyramids of marble and alabaster, with this inscription :—

Sacred to the Memory of

Sir CHRISTOPHER HATTON, *son of* WILLIAM, *grandson of* JOHN, *one of the most ancient family of the* HATTONS; *one of the fifty Gentlemen Pensioners to Her Majesty Queen* ELIZA-BETH; *Gentleman of the Privy-Chamber; Captain of the Guards; one of the Privy-Council, and High Chancellor of England, and of the University of Oxford: Who to the great grief of his Sovereign, and of all good men, ended his life religiously, after having lived unmarried to the age of* 51, *at his house in Holbourn, on the* 20th *of November*, A.D. 1591.

WILLIAM HATTON, *Knight, his nephew by the sister's side, and by adoption his son and heir, most sorrowfully raised this Tomb, a mark of his duty.*

On the left hand is the marble monument of *William Herbert*, Earl of *Pembroke*, and his lady; and near it, that of *John*, Duke of *Lancaster*, with this inscription :—

𝔥𝔢𝔯𝔢 𝔖𝔩𝔢𝔢𝔭𝔰 𝔦𝔫 𝔱𝔥𝔢 𝔏𝔬𝔯𝔡, 𝔍𝔬𝔥𝔫 𝔬𝔣 𝔊𝔞𝔫𝔱,

so called from the city of the same name in Flanders, where he was born, fourth son of EDWARD III., *King of England, and created by his father,* EARL OF RICHMOND. *He was thrice married: first to* BLANCH, *daughter and heiress of* HENRY, *Duke of* LANCASTER. *By her he received an immense inheritance, and became not only Duke of Lancaster, but* EARL OF LEICESTER, LINCOLN, *and* DERBY, *of whose race are descended many Emperors, Kings, Princes, and Nobles. His second wife was* CONSTANCE, *who is here buried, daughter and heiress of* PETER, *King of* CASTILE *and* LEON. *She brought him one only daughter,* CATHERINE, *of whom, by* HENRY *are descended the Kings of* SPAIN. *His third wife was* CATHERINE, *of a Knight's family, a woman of great beauty, by whom he had a numerous progeny; from which is descended, by the mother's side,* HENRY VII., *the most prudent King of England, by whose most happy marriage with* ELIZABETH, *daughter of* EDWARD IV., *of the line of* YORK, *the two royal lines of Lancaster and York are united, to the most desired tranquillity of England. The most illustrious Prince* JOHN, *surnamed* PLANTAGENET, *King of* CASTILE *and* LEON, *Duke of* LANCASTER, *Earl of* RICHMOND, LEICESTER, *and* DERBY, *Lieutenant of* AQUITAIN, *High-Stewart of* ENGLAND, *died in the* 21*st year of* RICHARD II., A.D. 1398.

A little farther, almost at the entrance of the Choir, in a certain recess, are two small stone chests, one of which is thus inscribed :—

𝔥𝔢𝔯𝔢 𝔩𝔦𝔢𝔰 𝔖𝔢𝔟𝔞, 𝔎𝔦𝔫𝔤 𝔬𝔣 𝔱𝔥𝔢 𝔈𝔞𝔰𝔱 𝔖𝔞𝔯𝔬𝔫𝔰, 𝔴𝔥𝔬 𝔴𝔞𝔰 𝔠𝔬𝔫𝔳𝔢𝔯𝔱𝔢𝔡 𝔱𝔬 𝔱𝔥𝔢 𝔣𝔞𝔦𝔱𝔥 𝔟𝔶 𝔖𝔱 𝔈𝔯𝔨𝔢𝔫𝔴𝔞𝔩𝔡, 𝔅𝔦𝔰𝔥𝔬𝔭 𝔬𝔣 𝔏𝔬𝔫𝔡𝔬𝔫. A.D. 677.

36

On the other :

Here lies Ethelred, King of the Angles, Son of King Edgar; on whom St Dunstan is said to have denounced vengeance, on his Coronation-Day, in the following Words :—

"In as much, as thou hast aspired to the Throne by "the Death of thy Brother, against whose Blood the "English, along with thy infamous Mother, conspired; "the Sword shall not pass from thy House: but rage "all the Days of thy Life, afflicting all thy generation, "till thy Kingdom shall be translated to another, whose "Manner and Language the People under thee knoweth "not. Nor shall thy sin be done away till after long "Chastisement, nor the sin of thy Mother, nor the sin "of those Men who assisted in thy Wicked Council."

All which came to pass, as predicted by the Saint; for after being worsted and put to flight by *Sueno*, king of the *Danes*, and his son *Canute*, and at last closely besieged in *London*, he died miserably A.D. 1017, after he had reigned 36 years in great difficulties.

There is, besides, in the middle of the church, a tomb made of brass, of some Bishop of *London* named *William*, who was in favour of *Edward*, King of *England*, and afterwards was made counsellor to King *William*. He was Bishop 16 years, and died A.D. 1077. Near this is the following inscription :—

Virtue survives the Funeral.
To the Memory of
Thomas Linacre, an eminent Physician,
John Caius placed this Monument.

37

On the lower part of it, is this inscription in gold letters :

THOMAS LINACRE, *Physician to King* HENRY VIII., *a man learned in the Greek and Latin Languages, and particularly skilful in Physic, by which he restored many from a state of Languishment and Despair to Life.   He translated with extraordinary Eloquence many of* GALEN'S *Works into Latin; and published, a little before his death, at the request of his Friends, a very valuable book on the Correct Structure of the Latin Tongue.   He founded in perpetuity, in favour of Students in Physick, two Public Lectures at Oxford, and one at Cambridge.   In this city he brought about, by his own industry, the establishing of a College of Physicians, of which he was elected the first President.   He was a detester of all fraud and deceit, and faithful in his friendships; equally dear to men of all ranks.   He went into Orders a few years before his Death, and quitted this life full of years, and much lamented,* A.D. 1524, *on the 20th of October.*

There are many Tombs in this Church, but without any inscriptions.   It has a very fine organ, which, at Evening Prayer, accompanied with other instruments, is delightful.

In the Suburb to the west, joined to the City by a continued row of Palaces belonging to the chief Nobility, of a mile in length, and lying on the side next the *Thames*, is the small town of WESTMINSTER; originally called *Thorney* from its Thorn Bushes, but now *Westminster*, from its aspect and its monastery.   The Church is remarkable for the Coronation and the Burial of the Kings of *England*.   Upon this spot is said formerly to have stood a Temple of *Apollo*, which was thrown down by an earthquake in the time of *Antoninus Pius;* from the ruins of which *Sebert*, King of the *East-Saxons*, erected another to *St Peter*.   This was subverted by the *Danes*, and again renewed by Bishop *Dunstan*, who gave it to a few monks.   Afterwards, King

Edward the Confessor built it entirely new, with the tenth of his whole revenue, to be the place of his own burial, and a convent of *Benedictine* monks; and enriched it with estates dispersed all over *England.* In this Church the following things are worthy of notice :

In the first Choir, the Tomb of *Anne of Cleves*, wife of *Henry VIII.*, without any inscription.

On the opposite side are two stone Sepulchres. First : *Edward*, Earl of *Lancaster*, brother of *Edward I.* Secondly : *Ademar* of *Valence*, Earl of *Pembroke*, son of *Ademar* of *Valence.* Joining to these is a third, of *Aveline*, Countess of *Lancaster.*

In the second Choir is the Chair on which the Kings are seated, when they are crowned ; in it is enclosed a stone, said to be that on which the Patriarch *Jacob* slept, when he dreamed he saw a ladder reaching quite up into Heaven. The following verses are written upon a Tablet hanging near it ; the sense of which is :

That if any Faith is to be given to ancient Chronicles, a stone of great note is enclosed in this Chair, being the same on which the Patriarch JACOB *reposed, when he beheld the miraculous descent of Angels.* EDWARD I., *the Mars and Hector of England, having conquered Scotland, brought it from thence.*

The Tomb of *Richard II.* and his wife, of brass gilt, and the verses written round it :

Perfect and Prudent, Richard by right the Second,
Vanquished by Fortune, lies here now graven in stone,
True of his Word, and thereto well resound ;
Seemly in Person, and like to Homer, as one
In worldly Prudence, and ever the Church in one
Upheld and favour'd, casting the Proud to ground,
And all that would his Royal State confound.

Without the Tomb is this inscription :

𝕳𝖊𝖗𝖊 𝖑𝖎𝖊𝖘 𝕶𝖎𝖓𝖌 𝕽𝖎𝖈𝖍𝖆𝖗𝖉, 𝖜𝖍𝖔 𝖕𝖊𝖗𝖎𝖘𝖍𝖊𝖉 𝖇𝖞 𝖆 𝖈𝖗𝖚𝖊𝖑 𝕯𝖊𝖆𝖙𝖍,
𝖎𝖓 𝖙𝖍𝖊 𝖄𝖊𝖆𝖗 1369.

To have been happy is additional misery.

Near him is the Monument of his Queen, daughter of the Emperor *Wenceslaus*. On the left hand is the Tomb of *Edward I.*, with this inscription :

𝕳𝖊𝖗𝖊 𝖑𝖎𝖊𝖘 𝕰𝖉𝖜𝖆𝖗𝖉 𝕴., 𝖜𝖍𝖔 𝖍𝖚𝖒𝖇𝖑𝖊𝖉 𝖙𝖍𝖊 𝕾𝖈𝖔𝖙𝖘. 𝕬.𝕯. 1308.

Be true to your engagements.

He reigned 46 years.

The Tomb of *Edward III.*, of copper gilt, with this Epitaph :

Of English Kings here lieth the beauteous Flower,
Of all before past, and Myrror to them shall sue :
A merciful King, of Peace Conservator,
The third EDWARD, *etc.*

Vid. DART. II. 44.

Beside the Tomb are these words :

𝕰𝖉𝖜𝖆𝖗𝖉 𝕴𝕴𝕴. 𝖜𝖍𝖔𝖘𝖊 𝖋𝖆𝖒𝖊 𝖍𝖆𝖘 𝖗𝖊𝖆𝖈𝖍'𝖉 𝖙𝖔 𝕳𝖊𝖆𝖛𝖊𝖓. 𝕬.𝕯. 1377.

Fight for your Country.

Here is shown his Sword, eight feet in length, which they say he used in the Conquest of *France*.

His Queen's Epitaph :

𝕳𝖊𝖗𝖊 𝖑𝖎𝖊𝖘 𝕼𝖚𝖊𝖊𝖓 𝕻𝖍𝖎𝖑𝖎𝖕𝖕𝖆, 𝖜𝖎𝖋𝖊 𝖔𝖋 𝕰𝖉𝖜𝖆𝖗𝖉 𝕴𝕴𝕴. 𝕬.𝕯. 1369.

Learn to live.

At a little distance, the Tomb of *Henry V.*, with this Legend :

Henry, the Scourge of France, lies in this Tomb. A.D. 1422.
Virtue subdues all things.

Near this lies the Coffin of *Catherine*, unburied, and to be opened by any one that pleases. On the outside is this inscription :

Fair Catherine is at length united to her Lord. A.D. 1437.
Shun idleness.

The Tomb of *Henry III.*, of brass gilt, with this Epitaph :

Henry III. the Founder of this Cathedral, A.D. 1273.
War is delightful to the inexperienced.

It was this *Henry* who, 160 years after *Edward the Confessor* had built this Church, took it down, and raised an entire new one of beautiful architecture, supported by rows of marble columns, and its roof covered with sheets of lead, a work of fifty years before its completion. It has been much enlarged at the West End by the Abbots. After the expulsion of the Monks, it experienced many changes : first it had a Dean and Prebendaries; then a Bishop, who having squandered the Revenues, resigned it again to a Dean. In a little time, the Monks with their Abbot were reinstated by Queen *Mary;* but they being soon ejected by authority of Parliament, it was converted into a Cathedral Church ; nay, into a Seminary for the Church by Queen *Elizabeth,* who instituted there twelve Prebendaries, an equal number of invalid Soldiers, and forty Scholars; who at a proper time were elected into the Universities, and are thence transplanted into the Church and State.

Next to be seen is the Tomb of *Eleanor*, daughter of *Alphonso*, King of *Spain*, and wife of *Edward I.*, with this inscription :

This Eleanor was Consort of Edward I. A.D. 1298.

Learn to die.

The Tomb of *Elizabeth*, daughter of *Henry VII.*

In the middle of this Chapel is the Shrine of *St Edward*, the last King of the *Saxons.* It is composed of marbles in *Mosaic;* round it runs this inscription in letters of gold :

The Venerable King, St Edward the Confessor,

A Heroe adorned with every Virtue.

He died on the fifth of January, 1065,

And Mounted into Heaven.

Lift up your hearts.

The third Choir, of surprising splendour and elegance, was added to the East End by *Henry VII.* for a Burying-place for himself and his posterity. Here is to be seen his magnificent Tomb, wrought of brass and marble, with this Epitaph :

Here lies Henry,

Seventh of that Name, formerly King of ENGLAND, *Son of* EDMUND, *Earl of* RICHMOND, *who, ascending the Throne on the 22d day of August, was Crowned on the 30th of October following, at Westminster, in the year of our Lord* 1485. *He died on the 21st of April, in the 53rd year of his age, after a Reign of 22 years and eight months, wanting a day.*

This monument is inclosed with Rails of Brass, with a long Epitaph in Latin verse.

Under the same Tomb lies buried *Edward VI.*, King of *England*, son of *Henry VIII.* by *Jane Seymour.* He succeeded to his Father when he was but nine years old, and died A.D. 1553, on the 6*th* of *July*, in the 16th year of his Age, and of his Reign the 7th, not without suspicion of Poison.

Mary was proclaimed Queen by the people on the 19th of July, and died in *November* 1558, and is buried in some corner of the same Choir, without any inscription.

Queen *Elizabeth.*

Here lies Queen Elizabeth,

Daughter of EDWARD IV., *Sister of King* EDWARD V., *Wife of* HENRY VII., *and the glorious Mother of* HENRY VIII. *She died in the Tower of London, on the* 11*th of February, A.D.* 1502, *in the* 37*th year of her Age.*

Between the second and third Choirs, in the side Chapels, are the Tombs of *Sebert*, King of the the *East-Saxons*, who built this Church with stone; and of

Margaret of Richmond,

Mother of HENRY VII., *Grandmother of* HENRY VIII. *She gave this Monastery to the Monks of* WINBOURNE,* *who preached and taught Grammar all England over, and appointed Salaries to two Professors of Divinity, one at* OXFORD, *another at* CAMBRIDGE, *where she founded two Colleges, to* CHRIST, *and to* JOHN *his Disciple. She died A.D.* 1463, *on the 3rd of the Calends of July.*

And of *Margaret*, Countess of *Lenox*, Grandmother of *James VI.* King of *Scotland.*

---

* This is a mistake. Her Epitaph says: "Stipendia constituit tribus hoc cænobio Monachis et Doctori Grammatices apud Wymbourne."

William of *Valence*, half-brother of *Henry III.*

The Earl of *Cornwall*, brother of *Edward III.*

Upon another Tomb is an honorary inscription for *Francis*, Duchess of *Suffolk*. The sense of it is—

> *That Title, Royal Birth, Riches, or a large Family, are of*
>   *no avail:*
> *That all are Transitory; Virtue alone resisting the Funeral*
>   *Pile.*
> *That this Lady was first Married to a Duke; then to* STOKE,
>   *a Gentleman;*
> *And lastly, by the grave Espoused to Christ.*

The next is the Tomb of Lord *Russel*, Son of the Earl of *Bedford*, whose Lady composed the following *Greek* and *Latin* verses, and had them engraved on marble:

> *How was I startled at the cruel Feast,*
> *By Death's rude Hands in horrid manner drest;*
> *Such Grief as sure no hapless Woman knew,*
> *When thy pale Image lay before my view.*
> *Thy Father's heir in beauteous Form array'd*
> *Like Flowers in Spring, and fair, like them to fade;*
> *Leaving behind unhappy wretched me,*
> *And all my little Orphan-progeny;*
> *Alike the beauteous Face, the comely air,*
> *The Tongue persuasive, and the Action fair,*
> *Decay: So Learning too in Time shall waste;*
> *But Faith, Chaste lovely Faith, shall ever last.*
> *The one bright Glory of this House, the Pride*
> *Of all his Country, dusty Ruins hide:*
> *Mourn, hapless Orphans, mourn, once happy Wife,*
> *For when he dy'd, dy'd all the Joys of Life.*

Pious and Just, amidst a large Estate,
He got at once the Name of Good and Great.
He made no flattering Parasite his Guest,
But asked the good Companions to the Feast.

Anne, Countess of *Oxford,* Daughter of *William Cecil,* Baron *Burleigh,* and Lord Treasurer.

Philippa, Daughter and Coheiress of *John,* Lord *Mohun* of *Dunster,* Wife of *Edward,* Duke of *York.*

Frances, Countess of *Sussex,* of the antient Family of *Sidney.*

Thomas Bromley, Chancellor to Queen *Elizabeth.*

The Earl of *Bridgwater,* Lord *Dawbney,* Lord Chamberlain to *Henry VII.* and his Lady.

And thus much for WESTMINSTER.

There are many other Churches in this City; but none so remarkable for Tombs of Persons of Distinction.

Near to this Church is *Westminster Hall,* where, besides the Sessions of Parliament, which are often held there, are the Courts of Justice; and at stated times are heard there Trials in Law, or concerning the King's Patrimony; or in Chancery, which moderates the severity of the Common Law by Equity. Till the time of *Henry I.,* the prime Court of Justice was moveable, and followed the King's Court; but he enacted, by the MAGNA CHARTA, *That the Common Pleas should no longer attend his Court, but be held at some determined Place.* The present Hall was built by King *Richard II.,* in the place of an ancient one, which he caused to be taken down. He made it part of his Habitation (for at that time the Kings of *England* determined Causes in their own proper Person, and from the days of *Edward* the Confessor, had their Palace adjoining), till about 60 years since, upon its being burnt,

Henry VIII. removed the Royal residence to *Whitehall,* situated in the neighbourhood, which a little before was the House of Cardinal *Wolsey:* This Palace is truly Royal; inclosed on one side by the *Thames,* on the other by a Park, which connects it with St *James's,* another Royal Palace. In the Chamber where the Parliament is usually held, the Seats and Wainscot are made of Wood, *the Growth of Ireland;* said to have that occult property that all poisonous animals are driven away by it; and it is affirmed for certain, that in *Ireland* there are neither Serpents, Toads, nor any other Venomous Creature to be found. Near this Palace are seen an immense number of Swans, who wander up and down the river for some miles, in great security; nobody daring to molest, much less kill any of them, under Penalty of a considerable Fine.

In *Whitehall* are the following things worthy of observation :—

(I.) The Royal Library, well stored with *Greek, Latin, Italian,* and *French* books : Amongst the rest, a little one in French, upon Parchment, in the handwriting of the present reigning Queen *Elizabeth,* thus inscribed :

> *To the most High, Puissant, and redoubted Prince,* HENRY VIII., *of the name, King of* ENGLAND, FRANCE, *and* IRELAND, *Defender of the Faith:* ELIZABETH, *his most humble Daughter, Health and Obedience.*

All these Books are bound in Velvet of different Colours, though chiefly red, with Clasps of Gold and Silver; some have Pearls, and precious Stones set in their Bindings.

(II.) Two little Silver Cabinets of Exquisite Work, in which the Queen keeps her paper, and which she uses for Writing Boxes.

(III.) The Queen's Bed, ingeniously composed of Woods of different Colours; with Quilts of Silk, Velvet, Gold, Silver, and Embroidery.

(IV.) A little Chest, ornamented all over with Pearls, in which

46

the Queen keeps her Bracelets, Ear-rings, and other things of extraordinary value.

(V.) Christ's passion, in painted Glass.

(VI.) Portraits, among which are—Queen ELIZABETH, at 16 years old. HENRY, RICHARD, EDWARD, Kings of ENGLAND; ROSAMOND; LUCRECE, a Grecian Bride, in her Nuptial Habit; the Genealogy of the Kings of ENGLAND; a Picture of King EDWARD VI., representing at first sight something quite deformed, till by looking through a small Hole in the Cover, which is put over it, you see it in its true Proportions; CHARLES V., Emperor; CHARLES EMANUEL, Duke of *Savoy*, and CATHERINE of *Spain*, his Wife; FERDINAND, Duke of *Florence*, with his Daughters; one of PHILIP, King of *Spain*, when he came into *England* and married MARY; HENRY VII., HENRY VIII., and his Mother: Besides many more of illustrious Men and Women; and a Picture of the Siege of *Malta*.

(VII.) A small Hermitage, half hid in a Rock, finely Carved in Wood.

(VIII.) Variety of Emblems, on Paper, cut in the Shape of Shields, with Mottoes, used by the Nobility at Tilts and Tournaments, hung up here for a Memorial.

(IX.) Different Instruments of Music, upon one of which two Persons may perform at the same Time.

(X.) A Piece of Clock-work, an *Aethiop* riding upon a Rhinoceros, with four attendants, who all make their obeisance, when it strikes the Hour; these are all put into motion by winding up the machine.

At the Entrance into the Park, from *Whitehall*, is this inscription :—

> *The Fisherman who has been wounded, learns, though late, to*
> *beware;*
> *But the unfortunate* Actaeon *always presses on.   The Chaste*
> *Virgin naturally pitied:*
> *But the powerful Goddess revenged the Wrong.*

Let Actaeon *fall a prey to his Dogs.*
An Example to Youth,
A Disgrace to those that belong to him !
May Diana *live the Care of Heaven;*
The Delight of Mortals;
*The security of those that belong to her!**

In this Park is great plenty of Deer.

In a Garden joining to this Palace, there is a *Jet d'eau*, with a Sun-dial, which, while strangers are looking at it, a quantity of Water, forced by a Wheel, which the Gardiner turns at a distance, through a number of little Pipes, plentifully sprinkles those that are standing round.

GUILDHALL, a fine Structure. built by THOMAS KNOWLES : Here are to be seen the Statues of two Giants, said to have assisted the *English* when the *Romans* made war upon them; CORINIUS of *Britain*, and GOGMAGOG of *Albion*. Beneath, upon a Table, the Titles of CHARLES V., Emperor, are written in Letters of Gold.

The Government of *London* is this :

The City is divided into 25 Regions, or Wards; the Council is composed of 24 Aldermen. one of which presides over every Ward. And whereas of old the Chief Magistrate was a Portreve, *i.e.*, Governor of the City: RICHARD I. appointed two Bailiffs; instead of which, King JOHN gave a power by Grant, of chusing annually a Mayor, from any of the twelve principal Companies, and to name two Sheriffs, one of which to be called the King's, the other, the City's. It is scarce credible how this City increased, both in public and private Buildings, upon Establishing this form of Government. —Vide *Cambden's Britan., Middlesex.*

It is worthy of observation, that every year, upon St. BARTHOLE-

---

* This romantic Inscription probably alluded to PHILIP II., who wooed the Queen after her Sister's Death ; and to the Destruction of his Armada.

MEW's Day, when the Fair is held, it is usual for the Mayor, attended by the 12 principal Aldermen, to walk in a neighbouring Field, dressed in his Scarlet Gown, and about his neck a Golden Chain, to which is hung a Golden Fleece, and besides, that particular Ornament, which distinguishes the most noble Order of the Garter. During the year of his magistracy, he is obliged to live so magnificently, that Foreigner or Native, without any Expence, is free, if he can find a chair empty, to Dine at his table, where there is always the greatest Plenty. When the Mayor goes out of the Precincts of the City, a Scepter, a Sword, and a Cap, are borne before him, and he is followed by the principal Aldermen in Scarlet Gowns, with Gold Chains; himself and they on Horseback : upon their arrival at a place appointed for that Purpose, where a Tent is pitched, the Mob begin to wrestle before them, two at a time; the Conquerors receive Rewards from the Magistrates. After this is over, a Parcel of live Rabbits are turned loose among the Crowd, which are pursued by a number of Boys, who endeavour to catch them, with all the noise they can make. While we were at this Show, one of our Company, TOBIAS SALANDER, Doctor of Physic, had his Pocket picked of his Purse, with nine Crowns *du soleil*, which, without doubt, was so cleverly taken from him, by an *Englishman* who always kept very close to him, that the Doctor did not in the least perceive it.

The *Castle*, or TOWER of LONDON, called *Bringwin*, and *Tourgwin*, in *Welch*, from its whiteness, is encompassed by a very deep and broad Ditch, as well as a double Wall very high. In the middle of the whole is that very antient and very strong Tower, enclosed with four others, which, in the opinion of some, was built by JULIUS CAESAR. Upon entering the TOWER, we were obliged to quit our swords at the Gate, and deliver them to the Guard. When we were introduced, we were shown a hundred pieces of Arras belonging to the Crown, made of Gold, Silver, and Silk; several Saddles, covered

49

with Velvet of different Colours; an immense quantity of Bed-furniture, such as Canopies, and the like, some of them most richly ornamented with Pearl; some Royal Dresses, so extremely magnificent, as to raise any one's admiration at the sums they must have cost. We were next led into the Armoury, in which are these particularities: Spears, out of which you may shoot; Shields, that will give fire four times; a great many rich Halberds, commonly called Partuisans, with which the Guard defend the Royal Person in battle; some Lances, covered with red and green Velvet, and the body armour of HENRY VIII.; many, and very beautiful Arms, as well for Men, as for Horses in horse-fights; the Lance of CHARLES BRANDON, Duke of SUFFOLK, three spans thick; two pieces of Cannon, the one fires three, the other seven Balls at a time; two others, made of Wood, which the *English* had at the siege of *Boulogne*, in *France*, and by this stratagem, without which they could not have succeeded, they struck a terror into the inhabitants, as at the appearance of Artillery, and the Town was surrendered upon Articles; 19 Cannon, of a thicker make than ordinary, and in a Room apart; 36 of a smaller; other Cannon for Chain-shot; and Balls proper to bring down Masts of Ships. Cross-bows, Bows and Arrows, of which to this day the English make great use in their Exercises: but who can relate all that is to be seen here? Eight or nine men, employed by the year, are scarcely sufficient to keep all the Arms bright.

The Mint for Coining Money is in the Tower.

N.B.—It is to be noted that when any of the nobility are sent hither, on the charge of high crimes, punishable with death, such as Treason, etc., they seldom or never recover their liberty. Here was beheaded ANNA BOLEN, Wife of King HENRY VIII., and lies buried in the Chapel, but without any inscription; and Queen ELIZABETH was kept prisoner here by her sister, Queen MARY, at whose death she was Enlarged and by right called to the Throne.

On coming out of the Tower, we were led to a small House close by, where are kept variety of Creatures, *viz.:* three Lionesses, one Lion of great size, called EDWARD VI., from his having been born in that reign; a Tygar; a Lynx; a Wolf, excessively old : this is a very scarce animal in *England*, so that their Sheep and Cattle stray about in great numbers, free from any Danger, though without anybody to keep them; there is, besides, a Porcupine, and an Eagle : all these Creatures are kept in a remote place, fitted up for the purpose, with wooden lattices, at the Queen's expence.

Near to this Tower, is a large open space : on the highest part of it is erected a wooden Scaffold, for the execution of Noble Criminals; upon which, they say, three Princes of England, the last of their Families, have been beheaded for High Treason.

On the Bank of the Thames, close by, are a great many Cannon, such, chiefly, as are used at Sea.

The next thing worthy of note, is the ROYAL EXCHANGE, so named by Queen ELIZABETH, built by Sir THOMAS GRESHAM, Citizen, for public ornament, and the convenience of Merchants. It has a great effect, whether you consider the stateliness of the building, the assemblage of different nations, or the quantity of merchandise. I shall say nothing of the hall belonging to the *Hans Society;* or of the Conveyance of Water to all parts of the Town by subterraneous pipes, nor the beautiful conduits and cisterns for the reception of it; nor of the rising of water out of the Thames by a wheel, invented a few years since by a German.

BRIDEWELL, at present the House of Correction : It was built in six weeks for the reception of the Emperor CHARLES V.

A HALL, built by a Cobler, and bestowed on the City, where are exposed to Sale, three times in a week, Corn, Wool, Cloth, Fruits, and the like.

Without the City are some *Theatres*, where *English* actors represent almost every day tragedies and comedies to very numerous

Audiences; these are concluded with Music, variety of Dances, and the excessive applause of those that are present.

Not far from one of these Theatres, which are built of Wood, lies the Royal Barge, close to the River; it has two splendid Cabbins, beautifully ornamented with Glass Windows, Painting, and Gilding; it is kept upon dry Ground, and sheltered from the weather.

There is still another place, built in the form of a Theatre, which serves for the baiting of Bulls and Bears; they are fastened behind, and then worried by great *English* bull-dogs; but not without great risque to the dogs, from the horns of the one, and the teeth of the other; and it sometimes happens they are killed upon the spot; fresh ones are immediately supplied in the place of those that are wounded or tired. To this entertainment, there often follows that of whipping a blinded bear, which is performed by five or six men, standing circularly with whips, which they exercise upon him without mercy, as he cannot escape from them because of his chain; he defends himself with all his force and skill, throwing down all who come within his reach, and are not active enough to get out of it, and tearing the whips out of their hands, and breaking them. At these spectacles, and everywhere else, the *English* are constantly smoaking tobacco, and in this manner: they have pipes on purpose made of clay, into the farther end of which they put the Herb, so dry that it may be rubbed into powder, and putting fire to it, they draw the smoke into their mouths, which they puff out again, through their nostrils, like funnels, along with it plenty of phlegm and defluxion from the head. In these theatres, fruits, such as apples, pears, and nuts, according to the season, are carried about to be sold, as well as ale and wine.

There are fifteen *Colleges*, within and without the City, nobly built, with beautiful gardens adjoining; of these, the three principal are :—

(I.) The TEMPLE, inhabited formerly by the Knights Templars:

It seems to have taken its name from the old Temple, or Church, which has a round Tower added to it, under which lie buried those Kings of *Denmark*, that reigned in *England*.

(II.) GRAYS-INN.   And,

(III.) LINCOLNS-INN.

In these Colleges numbers of the young nobility, gentry, and others, are educated, and chiefly in the study of Physic, for very few apply themselves to that of the Law : They are allowed a very good Table, and silver cups to drink out of.   Once a person of distinction, who could not help being surprised at the great number of cups, said, He should have thought it more suitable to the life of students, if they had used rather Glass, or Earthenware, than Silver.   The College answered, They were ready to make him a present of all their plate, provided he would undertake to supply them with all the glass and earthenware they should have a demand for; since it was very likely he would find the expence, from constant breaking, exceed the value of the silver.

The Streets in this City are very handsome and clean ; but that which is named from the Gold-smiths, who inhabit it, surpasses all the rest : There is in it a gilt tower, with a fountain that plays; near it, on the farther side, is a handsome house, built by a Goldsmith, and presented by him to the City.   There are, besides, to be seen in this street, as in all others where there are Goldsmiths' shops, all sorts of gold and silver vessels exposed to sale ; as well as ancient and modern medals, in such quantities as must surprise a man the first time he sees and considers them.

FITZ-STEPHENS, a writer of *English* History, reckoned in his time, in *London*, 127 Parish Churches, and 13 belonging to Convents. He mentions, besides, that upon a review there of men able to bear arms, the People brought into the Field under their Colours, 40,000 Foot, and 20,000 Horse.—Vide *Cambden's Britan. Middlesex.*

The best *Oysters* are sold here in great quantities.   Every body

53

knows that English Cloth is much approved of, for the goodness of the materials, and imported into all the Kingdoms and Provinces of *Europe*.

We were shewn at the House of *Leonard Smith*, a Taylor, a most perfect looking-glass, ornamented with Gold, Pearl, Silver, and Velvet, so richly, as to be estimated at five hundred *Ecus du Soleil*. We saw at the same place the Hippocamp and Eagle Stone, both very curious and rare.

And thus much for LONDON.

UPON taking the Air down the River, the first Thing that struck us, was the Ship of that noble Pirate, *Sir Francis Drake*, in which he is said to have surrounded this Globe of Earth. On the left Hand lies *Radcliffe*, a considerable Suburb: on the opposite Shore is fixed a long Pole with Ram's-horns upon it, the Intention of·which was vulgarly said to be, a Reflection upon wilful and contented Cuckolds.

We arrived next at the Royal Palace of *Greenwich*, reported to have been originally built by *Humphrey*, Duke of *Gloucester*, and to have received very magnificent Additions from *Henry VII*. It was here *Elizabeth*, the present Queen, was born, and here she generally resides; particularly in Summer, for the Delightfulness of its Situation. We were admitted, by an Order Mr Rogers had procured from the Lord Chamberlain, into the Presence-Chamber, hung with rich Tapestry, and the Floor, after the English Fashion, strewed with Hay,* through which the Queen commonly passes on her way to Chapel. At the Door stood a Gentleman dressed in Velvet, with a Gold Chain, whose Office was to introduce to the Queen any Person of Distinction, that came to wait on her. It was Sunday

---

* He probably means Rushes.

when there is usually the greatest Attendance of Nobility. In the same Hall were the *Archbishop of Canterbury*, the *Bishop of London*, a great number of Counsellors of State, Officers of the Crown, and Gentlemen, who waited the Queen's coming out; which she did from her own Apartment, when it was Time to go to Prayers, attended in the following manner:

First went Gentlemen, Barons, Earls, Knights of the Garter, all richly dressed and bareheaded; *next* came the Chancellor, bearing the Seals in a red-silk Purse, between Two: one of which carried the Royal Sceptre, the other the Sword of State, in a red Scabbard, studded with golden Fleur-de-Lis, the Point upwards; *next* came THE QUEEN, in the Sixty-fifth Year of her Age, as we were told, very Majestic; her Face oblong, fair, but wrinkled; her Eyes small, yet black and pleasant; her Nose a little hooked; her Lips narrow; and her Teeth black (a Defect the English seem subject to, from their too great Use of Sugar); she had in her Ears two Pearls, with very rich Drops; she wore false Hair, and that red; upon her Head she had a small Crown, reported to be made of some of the Gold of the celebrated *Lunebourg Table;* * her Bosom was uncovered, as all the *English* Ladies have it, till they marry; and she had on a Necklace of exceeding fine Jewels; her Hands were small, her Fingers long, and her Stature neither tall nor low; her Air was stately, her Manner of speaking mild and obliging. That Day she was dressed in white Silk, bordered with Pearls of the Size of Beans, and over it a Mantle of black Silk, shot with Silver Threads; her Train was very long, the End of it borne by a Marchioness; instead of a Chain, she had an oblong Collar of Gold and Jewels. As she went along in all this State and Magnificence, she spoke very graciously, first to one, then to another, whether foreign Ministers, or those who attended for different Reasons, in English, French, and Italian; for, besides

---

* At this distance of time, it is difficult to say what this was.

being well skilled in Greek, Latin, and the Languages I have mentioned, she is Mistress of Spanish, Scotch, and Dutch. Whoever
speaks to her, it is kneeling; now and then she raises some with her
Hand. While we were there, *W. Slawata*, a Bohemian Baron, had
Letters to present to her; and she, after pulling off her Glove, gave
him her right Hand to kiss, sparkling with Rings and Jewels, a mark
of particular Favour. Wherever she turned her Face, as she was
going along, everybody fell down on their knees.* The Ladies of
the Court followed next to her, very handsome and well-shaped, and
for the most Part dressed in white; she was guarded on each Side
by the Gentlemen Pensioners, fifty in number, with gilt Battle-axes.
In the Anti-chapel, next the Hall where we were, Petitions were
presented to her, and she received them most graciously, which
occasioned the Acclamation of, *Long live Queen Elizabeth!* She
answered it with, *I thank you, my good People.* In the Chapel
was excellent Music; as soon as it and the Service was over, which
scarce exceeded half an Hour, the Queen returned in the same State
and Order, and prepared to go to Dinner. But while she was still
at Prayers, we saw her Table set out with the following Solemnity.

A Gentleman entered the Room bearing a Rod, and along with
him another who had a Table-cloth, which, after they had both
kneeled three Times with the utmost Veneration, he spread upon
the Table, and after kneeling again, they both retired. Then came
two others, one with the Rod again, the other with a Salt-sellar, a
Plate, and Bread; when they had kneeled, as the others had done,
and placed what was brought upon the Table, they too retired with
the same Ceremonies performed by the first. At last came an

---

* Her father had been treated with the same deference. It is mentioned by
Fox, in his Acts and Monuments, that, when the Lord Chancellor went to appre-
hend Queen Catherine Parr, he spoke to the King on his knees.

King James I. suffered his courtiers to omit it.

—*Bacon's Papers, Vol. II., p. 516.*

unmarried Lady (we were told she was a Countess), and along with her a married one, bearing a Tasting-knife; the former was dressed in white Silk, who, when she had prostrated herself three Times, in the most graceful Manner, approached the Table, and rubbed the Plates with Bread and Salt, with as much Awe, as if the Queen had been present. When they had waited there a little while, the Yeomen of the Guard entered, bare-headed, cloathed in Scarlet, with a golden Rose upon their Backs, bringing in at each Turn a Course of twenty-four Dishes, served in Plate most of it Gilt; these Dishes were received by a Gentleman in the same Order they were brought, and placed upon the Table, while the Lady-taster gave to each of the Guard a mouthful to Eat, of the particular Dish he had brought, for Fear of any Poison. During the Time that this Guard, which consists of the tallest and stoutest Men that can be found in all England—being carefully selected for this Service—were bringing Dinner, twelve Trumpets and two Kettle-drums made the Hall ring for half an Hour together. At the End of this Ceremonial a Number of unmarried Ladies appeared, who, with particular Solemnity, lifted the Meat off the Table, and conveyed it into the Queen's inner and more private Chamber, where, after she had chosen for herself, the rest goes to the Ladies of the Court.

The Queen dines and sups alone, with very few attendance; and it is very seldom that anybody, Foreigner or Native, is admitted at that Time, and then only at the intercession of somebody in power.

Near this Palace is the Queen's Park, stocked with Deer. Such Parks are common throughout England, belonging to those who are distinguished either for their Rank or Riches. In the middle of this is an old square Tower, called *Mirefleur*, supposed to be that mentioned in the Romance of *Amadis de Gaul;* and joining to it a Plain, where Knights and other Gentlemen used to meet at set Times and Holidays to Exercise on Horseback.

We left *London* in a Coach, in order to see the remarkable Places in the Neighbourhood.

The first was THEOBALDS, belonging to Lord *Burleigh*, the Treasurer. In the Gallery was painted the Genealogy of the Kings of *England;* from this place, one goes into the Garden, encompassed with a Ditch full of Water, large enough for one to have the pleasure of going into a Boat, and rowing between the shrubs; here are great varieties of Trees and Plants, Labyrinths made with a great deal of Labour; a *Jet d'eau*, with its Bason of white Marble; and Columns and Pyramids of Wood and other Materials up and down the Garden. After seeing these, we were led by the Gardener into a Summer-house, in the lower part of which, built semi-circularly, are the twelve Roman Emperors, in Marble, and a Table of Touchstone; the upper part of it is set round with Cisterns of Lead, into which the Water is conveyed by Pipes, so that Fish may be kept in them; and in Summer time they are very convenient for Bathing. In another Room, for Entertainment, very near this, and joined to it by a little Bridge, was an Oval Table of red Marble. We were not admitted to see the Apartments of this Palace, there being nobody to shew it, as the Family was in Town attending the Funeral of their Lord.*

HODSON, a Village.

WARE, a Market Town.

PUCKERIDGE, a Village; this was the first place where we observed that the Beds at Inns were made by the Waiters.

CAMBORETUM, CANTABRIGIUM, and CANTABRIGIA, now called CAMBRIDGE, a celebrated Town, so named from the river *Cam*, which, after washing the western side, playing through Islands, turns to the east, and divides the Town into two parts, which are joined by a Bridge; whence its modern name. Formerly it had the Saxon one of GRANTBRIDGE. Beyond this Bridge is an antient and large

---

* Lord Treasurer Burleigh died August 4, 1598.

Castle, said to be built by the *Danes:* on this side, where far the greater part of the Town stands, all is splendid; the Streets fine, the Churches numerous, and those Seats of the Muses, the Colleges, most beautiful; in these, a great number of learned Men are supported, and the studies of all polite Sciences and Languages flourish. I think proper to mention some few things about the Foundation of this University and its Colleges. *Cantabar,* a *Spaniard,* is thought to have first instituted this University, 375 years before Christ; and *Sebert,* King of the *East-Angles,* to have restored it, A.D. 630. It was afterwards subverted in the Confusion under the *Danes,* and lay long neglected; till, upon the *Norman* Conquest, everything began to brighten up again. From that time, Inns and Halls for the Convenient Lodging of Students began to be built, but without any Revenues attached to them. The first College, called PETER-HOUSE, was built and endowed by *Hugh Balsam,* Bishop of *Ely,* A.D. 1280; and, in imitation of him, *Richard Badew,* with the assistance of *Elizabeth Burk,* Countess of *Clare* and *Ulster,* founded CLAER-HALL, in 1326; *Mary de St. Paul,* Countess of *Pembroke,* PEMBROKE-HALL, in 1343; the Monks of *Corpus Christi,* the College of the same name, though it has besides that of BENNET; *John Craudene,* TRINITY-HALL, 1354; *Edmond Gonville,* in 1348; and *John Caius,* a Physician in our times, GONVILLE and CAIUS COLLEGE; King *Henry VI.,* KING'S COLLEGE, in 1441; adding to it a Chapel, that may justly claim a place among the most beautiful buildings in the world; on its right side is a fine Library, where we saw the Book of Psalms in Manuscript upon Parchment, four spans in length, and three broad, taken from the Spaniards at the Siege of Cadiz, and thence brought into *England,* with other rich spoils. *Margaret* of *Anjou,* his wife, founded QUEEN'S COLLEGE, 1448. At the same time that *John Alcock,* Bishop of *Ely,* built JESUS COLLEGE; *Robert Woodlarke,* CATHERINE-HALL, 1456; *Margaret* of *Richmond,* mother of *Henry VII.,* CHRIST'S and ST. JOHN'S COLLEGES, about

1506; *Thomas Audley*, Chancellor of *England*, MAGDALEN COLLEGE, much increased since, both in buildings and revenue, by *Christopher Wray*, Lord Chief Justice; and the most potent King *Henry VIII.* erected TRINITY COLLEGE for Religion and Polite Letters; in its Chapel is the Tomb of Dr *Whitacre*, with an inscription in Gold Letters upon Marble; EMMANUEL COLLEGE, built in our own times by the most honourable and prudent Sir *Walter Mildmay*, one of Her Majesty's Privy Council; and, lastly, SIDNEY COLLEGE, now building by the Executors of the Lady *Frances Sidney*, Countess of *Sussex.**

We must note here that there is a certain sect in England called *Puritans.* These, according to the doctrine of the Church of *Geneva*, reject all ceremonies antiently held, and admit of neither organ nor Tombs in their places of Worship, and entirely abhor all difference in Rank among Churchmen, such as Bishops, Deans, etc. They were first named Puritans by the Jesuit *Sandys.* They do not live separate, but mix with those of the Church of England in the Colleges.

POTTON, a Village.

AMPTHILL, a Town; here we saw immense numbers of rabbits, which are reckoned as good as hares, and are very well tasted.

We passed through the towns of WOBURN, LEIGHTON, AILESBURY, and WHEATLEY.

Oxonium, OXFORD, the famed *Athens* of England; that glorious Seminary of Learning and Wisdom, whence Religion, Politeness, and Letters are abundantly dispersed into all parts of the Kingdom. The Town is remarkably fine, whether you consider the elegance of its private buildings, the magnificence of its Public ones, or the Beauty and Wholesomeness of its situation; which is on a

---

* She was the daughter, sister, and aunt of those eminent knights—Sir William, Sir Henry, and Sir Philip Sidney.

plain, encompassed in such a manner with Hills shaded with Wood, as to be sheltered on the one hand from the sickly South, and on the other from the blustering West, but open to the East that blows serene weather, and to the North the preventer of corruption; from which, in the opinion of some, it formerly obtained the appellation of *Bellositum*. This town is watered by two rivers, the *Cherwell*, and the *Isis*, vulgarly called the *Ouse;* and though these streams join in the same channel, yet the *Isis* runs more entire, and with more rapidity towards the south, retaining its name till it meets the *Thames*, which it seems long to have sought, at *Wallingford*, thence called by the compound name of *Thames*, it flows the Prince of all British Rivers; of whom we may justly say it both sows and waters *England*.

The Colleges in this University are as follow :—In the reign of *Henry III.*, *Walter Merton*, Bishop of *Rochester*, removed the College he had founded in Surrey, 1274, to *Oxford*, enriched it, and named it MERTON College; and soon after *William*, Archdeacon of *Durham*, restored, with additions, that building of *Alfred's*, now called UNIVERSITY College; in the reign of *Edward I.*, *John Baliol*, King of *Scotland*, or, as some will have it, his parents, founded BALIOL College. In the reign of *Edward II.*, *Walter Stapleton*, Bishop of *Exeter*, founded EXETER College, and HARTHALL; and, in imitation of him, the King, KING's College, commonly called ORIEL, and St. MARY's Hall. Next, *Philippa*, wife of Edward III., built QUEEN's College ; and *Simon Islip*, Archbishop of *Canterbury*, CANTERBURY College; *William Wickham*, Bishop of *Winchester*, raised that magnificent structure called NEW College. MAGDALEN College was built by *William Wainflet*, Bishop of *Winchester*, a noble Edifice, finely situated, and delightful for its walks. At the same time *Humphrey*, Duke of *Gloucester*, that great encourager of learning, built the Divinity School very splendidly, and over it a Library, to which he gave one hundred and twenty-nine very choice Books, purchased at a great price from *Italy*, but the Public has long since been robbed of the use of them by the avarice of Particulars. LINCOLN College; ALL-SOULS College; St. BERNARD's College; BRAZEN-NOSE College, founded by *William Smith*, Bishop of *Lincoln*, in the reign of *Henry VII.* Its revenues were augmented by *Alexander Nowell*, Dean of *St. Paul's, London;* upon the gate of this College is fixed a Nose of Brass. CORPUS CHRISTI College, built by *Richard Fox*, Bishop of *Winchester;* under his picture in the College Chapel are lines importing that it is the exact representation of his person and dress.

CHRIST'S College, the largest and most elegant of them all, was begun on the ground of *St. Frideswide's* Monastery by *Thomas Wolsey*, Cardinal of *York*, to which *Henry VIII.* joined *Canterbury* College, settled grant revenues upon it, and named it *Christ's* Church. The same great Prince, out of his own Treasury, to the Dignity of the Town, and Ornament of the University, made the one a Bishoprick, and instituted Professorships in the other.

JESUS College, built by *Hugh Price*, Doctor of Laws.

That fine edifice, the public schools, was entirely raised by Queen *Mary*, and adorned with various inscriptions.

Thus far of the Colleges and Halls, which for the beauty of their Buildings, their rich Endowments, and copious Libraries, excel all the academies in the Christian World. We shall add a little of the Academies themselves, and those that inhabit them.

There Students lead a life almost monastic, for as the monks had nothing in the world to do, but when they had said their prayers at stated hours, to employ themselves in instructive studies, no more have these. They are divided into Three Tables: the first is called the Fellows' Table, to which are admitted Earls, Barons, Gentlemen, Doctors, and Masters of Arts, but very few of the latter. This is more plentifully and expensively served than the others. The second is for Masters of Arts, Bachelors, some Gentlemen, and eminent Citizens. The third for people of low condition. While the rest are at dinner or supper in a great Hall, where they are all assembled, one of the Students reads aloud the Bible, which is placed on a desk in the middle of the Hall, and this office every one of them takes upon himself in his turn; as soon as grace is said after each meal, every one is at liberty either to retire to his own chambers, or to walk in the College Garden, there being none that has not a delightful one. Their Habit is almost the same as that of the Jesuits, their Gowns reaching down to their ancles, sometimes lined with fur, they wear square caps; the Doctors, Masters of Arts, and Professors have another kind of gown that distinguishes them. Every Student of any considerable standing has a key to the College Library, for no College is without one.

In an out part of the town, are the remains of a pretty large fortification, but quite in ruins. We were entertained at supper with an excellent Concert, composed of variety of Instruments. The next day we went as far as the Royal Palace of WOODSTOCK, where King *Ethelred* formerly held a Parliament, and enacted certain Laws. This Palace abounding in magnificence, was built by *Henry I.*, to which he joined a very large Park, enclosed with a Wall, according to *John Rosse* the first Park in *England.* In this very Palace the present reigning Queen *Elizabeth*, before she was confined to the Tower, was kept Prisoner by her Sister *Mary;* while she was detained here in the utmost peril of her life, she wrote with a piece of charcoal the following verses, composed by herself on a window-shutter:—

> " *O Fortune! how thy reckless wavering state,*
> *Hath fraught with cares my troubled wit!*
> *Witness this present Prison whither fate*
> *Hath borne me, and the joys I quit.*
> *Thou causedest the guilty to be loosed*
> *From bands, wherewith are Innocents inclosed;*
> *Causing the guiltless to be straight reserved,*
> *And freeing those that death had well deserved;*

But by her envy can be nothing wrought,
So God send to my Foes all they have thought."

A.D. M.D.L.V.   ELIZABETH, *Prisoner.*

Not far from this Palace are to be seen, near a spring of the brightest water, the Ruins of the Habitation of *Rosamund Clifford*, whose exquisite beauty so entirely captivated the heart of King *Henry II.*, that he lost the thought of all other women; she is said to have been poisoned at last by the Queen. All that remains of her Tomb of stone, the letters of which are almost worn out, is what follows:—

.   .   .   .   .   Adorent
Atque tibi detur requies, Rosamunda, precamur.

This rhyming Epitaph, likewise, was probably the work of some monk:—

"Hic jacet in tumba
Rosamundi non Rosamunda
Non redolet, sed olet,
Quae redolere solet."

Returning from thence to OXFORD, after dinner we proceeded on our journey, and passed through EWHELME, a Royal Palace, in which some almspeople are supported by an allowance from the Crown.

NETTLEBED, a Village.

We went through the little town of HENLEY; from hence the *Chiltern* Hills bear north in a continued ridge, and divide the counties of OXFORD and BUCKINGHAM.

We passed MAIDENHEAD.

WINDSOR, a Royal Castle, supposed to have been begun by King *Arthur*, its Buildings much increased by *Edward III.* The situation is entirely worthy of being a Royal Residence, a more beautiful being

64

scarce to be found. For from the brow of a gentle rising it enjoys the prospect of an even and green country; its front commands a valley extending every way, and chequered with arable lands and pasturage, cloathed up and down with Groves, and watered by that gentlest of Rivers, the *Thames;* behind rise several Hills, but neither steep nor very high, crowned with Woods, and seeming designed by Nature herself for the purpose of Hunting.

The Kings of ENGLAND, invited by the deliciousness of the place, very often retire hither ; and here was born the Conqueror of *France*, the glorious King *Edward III.*, who built the Castle new from the ground, and thoroughly fortified it with Trenches, and Towers of square stone, and having soon after subdued in battle *John* King of *France*, and *David* King of *Scotland*, he detained them both prisoners here at the same time. This Castle, besides being the Royal Palace, and having some magnificent Tombs of the Kings of *England*, is famous for the ceremonies belonging to the Knights of the Garter ; this order was instituted by *Edward III.*, the same who triumphed so illustriously over King *John* of *France*. The Knights of the Garter are strictly chosen for their military virtues, and antiquity of family. They are bound by solemn oath and vow to mutual and perpetual friendship among themselves, and to the not avoiding any danger whatever, or even death itself, to support by their joint endeavours the Honour of the Society; they are stiled, Companions of the Garter, from their wearing below the left knee a purple Garter, inscribed in letters of gold, with *Honi soit qui mal y pense—i.e.*, Evil to him who evil thinks : this they wear upon the left leg, in memory of one which happened to untie, was let fall by a great Lady, passionately loved by *Edward*, while she was dancing, and was immediately snatched up by the King; who to do honour to the Lady, not out of any trifling gallantry, but with a most serious and honourable purpose, dedicated it to the legs of the most distinguished nobility. The ceremonies of this Society are celebrated every year at WINDSOR, on *St. George's* day, the tutelar Saint of the Order, the King presiding; and the custom is, that the Knights Companions should hang up their helmet and shield, with their arms blazoned on it, in some conspicuous part of the Church.

There are three principal and very large Courts in WINDSOR Castle, which give great pleasure to the beholders; the first is enclosed with most elegant Buildings of white Stone, flat roofed, and covered with lead; here the Knights of the Garter are lodged; in the middle is a detached house, remarkable for its high tower, which the Governor inhabits; in this is the public Kitchen, well furnished with the proper utensils, besides a spacious Dining-room. where all the poor Knights eat at the same table; for into this Society of the Garter, the King and Sovereign elect, at his own choice, certain persons who must be gentlemen of three descents, and such as for their age and straitness of their fortunes, are fitter for saying their prayers, than for the service of War; to each of them is assigned a Pension of eighteen pounds per annum, and cloaths; the chief institution of so magnificent a foundation is, that they should say their daily prayers to God for the King's safety, and the happy administration of the Kingdom, to which purpose they attend the service, meeting twice every day at Chapel. The left side of this Court is ornamented by a most magnificent Chapel of one hundred and thirty-four paces in length, and sixteen in breadth; in this are eighteen seats fitted up in the time of *Edward III.*, for an equal number of Knights. This venerable building is decorated with the noble Monuments of *Edward IV., Henry VI.* and *VIII.*, and of his wife Queen *Jane.* It receives from the Royal liberality the annual income of two thousand pounds, and that still much encreased by the munificence of *Edward III.* and *Henry VII.* The greatest Princes in *Christendom* have taken it for the highest honour to be admitted into the Order of the Garter; and since its first institution, about twenty Kings, besides those of *England*, who are the Sovereigns of it, not to mention Dukes and persons of the greatest figure, have been of it. It consists of twenty-six companies.

In the inward Choir of the Chapel, are hung up sixteen Coats of Arms, Swords, and Banners, among which are those of *Charles V.* and *Rodolpus II.*, Emperors; of *Philip* of *Spain; Henry III.* of *France; Frederick II.* of *Denmark*, etc.; of *Casimer*, Count Palatine of the *Rhine;* and other Christian Princes, who have been chosen into this Order.

In the back Choir, or additional Chapel, are shewn Preparations made by Cardinal *Wolsey*, who was afterwards capitally * punished, for his own Tomb, consisting of eight large Brazen Columns placed round it, and nearer the Tomb four others in the shape of Candlesticks—the Tomb itself is of white and black Marble—all which are reserved, according to report, for the Funeral of *Queen Elizabeth.* The expenses already made for that purpose are estimated at upwards of £60,000. In the same Chapel is the Surcoat of *Edward III.*, and the Tomb of *Edward Fines*, Earl of *Lincoln*, Baron *Clinton* and *Say*, Knight of the most noble Order of the Garter, and formerly Lord High Admiral of *England.*

The second Court of WINDSOR Castle stands upon higher ground, and is enclosed with Walls of great strength, and beautified with fine Buildings, and a Tower; it was an antient Castle, of which old annals speak in this manner: King *Edward*, A.D. 1359, began a New Building in that part of the Castle of WINDSOR where he was born, for which reason he took care it should be decorated with larger and finer Edifices than the rest; in this Part were kept Prisoners *John*, King of *France*, and *David*, King of *Scots*, over whom *Edward* Triumphed at one and the same time. It was by their advice, struck with the advantage of its Situation, and with the

---

* This was a strange blunder to be made, so near the time, about so remarkable a person, unless he concluded that whoever displeased Henry VIII. was, of course, put to death.

Sums paid for their Ransom, that, by degrees, this Castle stretched to such magnificence, as to appear no longer a Fortress, but a Town of proper extent, and impregnable to any human Force; this particular part of the Castle was built at the Sole Expence of the, King of *Scotland*, except one Tower, which, from its having been Erected by the Bishop of *Winchester*, Prelate of the Order, is called WINCHESTER Tower,* there are a hundred steps to it, so ingeniously contrived, that horses can easily ascend them; it is an hundred and fifty paces in circuit; within it are preserved all manner of arms necessary for the defence of the place.

The third Court is much the largest of any, built at the Expence of the captive King of *France;* as it stands higher, so it greatly excels the two former in splendour and elegance; it is one hundred and forty-eight paces in length, and ninety-seven in breadth: in the middle of it is a Fountain of very clear Water, brought underground at an excessive Expence, from the distance of four Miles; towards the east are magnificent Apartments, destined for the Royal Household; towards the west is a Tennis Court, for the amusement of the Court; on the north side are the Royal Apartments, consisting of magnificent Chambers, Halls, and Bathing-rooms, consisting of a Private Chapel, the Roof of which is embellished with Golden Roses and *Fleur-de-lis;* in this, too, is that very large banquetting-room, seventy-eight paces long, and thirty wide, in which the Knights of the Garter annually celebrate the Memory of their tutelar Saint—*St. George*—with a Solemn and most Pompous Service. From hence runs a Walk of incredible beauty, three hundred and eighty paces in length, set round on every side with Supporters of Wood, which sustain a Balcony, from whence the Nobility and Persons of Distinction can take the pleasure of seeing Hunting and Hawking in a Lawn of sufficient space; for the Fields and Meadows,

---

* This is confounded with the round Tower.

clad with a variety of Plants and Flowers, swell gradually into Hills of perpetual Verdure quite up to the Castle, and at the bottom stretch out into an extended Plain, that strikes the Beholders with delight.

Besides what has been already mentioned, there are worthy of notice here, two Bathing-rooms, ceiled and wainscotted with Looking-glass; the Chamber in which *Henry VI.* was born; Queen *Elizabeth's* Bed-chamber, where is a Table of red Marble with white Streaks; a Gallery, everywhere ornamented with Emblems and Figures; a Chamber, in which are the Royal Beds of *Henry VII.* and his Queen, of *Edward VI.*, of *Henry VIII.* and of *Anne Bullen*, all of them eleven feet square, and covered with Quilts shining with Gold and Silver; Queen *Elizabeth's* Bed, with curious coverings of Embroidery, but not quite so long or large as the others; a Piece of Tapestry, in which is represented *Cloris*, King of *France*, with an Angel presenting to him the *Fleur-de-lis*, to be borne in his Arms; for before this time the Kings of *France* bore three Toads in their Shield, instead of which they afterwards placed three *Fleur-de-lis* on a blue field; this antique Tapestry is said to have been taken from a King of *France*, while the *English* were masters there. We were shewn there, among other things, the Horn of an Unicorn, of about eight spans and a half in length, valued at above £10,000; the Bird of Paradise, three spans long, three fingers broad, having a blue bill of the length of half an inch, the upper part of its head yellow, the nether part of an   colour; a little lower, from either side of its throat, stick out some reddish feathers, as well as from its back and the rest of its body; its wings, of a yellow colour, are twice as long as the Bird itself; from its back grow out length-ways two fibres or nerves, bigger at their ends, but like a pretty strong thread, of a leaden colour, inclining to black, with which, as it has no feet, it is said to fasten itself to trees, when it wants to rest; a Cushion most curiously wrought by Queen *Elizabeth's* own hands.

In the precincts of WINDSOR, on the other side the *Thames*, both whose banks are joined by a Bridge of Wood, is EATON, a well-built College, and famous School for Polite Letters, founded by *Henry VI.*, where, besides a Master, eight Fellows and Chanters, sixty Boys are maintained Gratis. They are taught Grammar, and remain in the School, till upon Trial made of their Genius and Progress in Study, they are sent to the University of CAMBRIDGE.

As we were returning to our Inn, we happened to meet some country People celebrating their Harvest-Home; their last load of Corn they Crown with Flowers, having besides an Image richly dressed, by which, perhaps, they would signify *Ceres*, this they keep moving about, while Men and Women, Men and Maid Servants, riding through the Streets in the Cart, shout as loud as they can, till they arrive at the Barn. The Farmers here do not bind up their Corn in Sheaves, as they do with us, but directly as they have Reaped or Mowed it, put it into Carts, and convey it into their Barns.

We went through the Town of STAINES.

HAMPTON COURT, a Royal Palace, magnificently Built with Brick, by Cardinal *Wolsey*, in ostentation of his Wealth, where he enclosed five very ample Courts, consisting of noble Edifices, in very beautiful work. Over the Gate in the Second Area is the Queen's Device—a Golden Rose—with this Motto: *Dieu et mon droit.* On the inward side of this Gate are the Effigies of the twelve *Roman* Emperors, in plaster. The chief Area is paved with square Stone; in its centre is a Fountain that throws up Water, covered with a gilt Crown, on the Top of which is a Statue of Justice, supported by Columns of black and white Marble. The Chapel of this Palace is most splendid, in which the Queen's Closet is most transparent, having its Windows of Chrystal. We were led into two Chambers, called the Presence, or Chambers of Audience, which shone with Tapestry of Gold and Silver and Silk of different colours. Under the Canopy of State are these Words, Embroidered in Pearl: *Vivat Henricus Octavus.* Here is, besides, a small Chapel, richly hung with Tapestry, where the Queen performs her Devotions. In her Bed-chamber the Bed was covered with very costly Coverlids of Silk. At no great distance from this Room we were shewn a Bed, the Tester of which was worked by *Anne Bullen*, and presented by her to her husband, *Henry VIII.* All the other Rooms, being very numerous, are adorned with Tapestry of Gold, Silver, and Velvet, in some of which were Woven History Pieces; in others, *Turkish* and *American* dresses, all extremely natural.

In the Hall are these Curiosities :—a very clear looking glass, ornamented with columns and little images of alabaster; a Portrait of *Edward VI.*, brother to Queen *Elizabeth;* the true portrait of *Lucretia;* a Picture of the Battle of *Pavia;* the history of Christ's Passion, carved in mother of pearl; the portraits of *Mary* Queen of *Scots*, who was beheaded, and her daughter; * the Picture of *Ferdinand*, Prince of *Spain;* and of *Philip*, his son; that of *Henry VIII.*, under it was placed the Bible curiously written upon parchment; an artificial sphere; several musical instruments; in the Tapestry are represented Negroes riding upon Elephants. The bed in which *Edward VI.* is said to have been born, and where his Mother *Jane Seymour* died in child-bed. In one chamber were several exceedingly rich Tapestries, which are hung up when the Queen gives audience to Foreign Ambassadors; there were numbers of cushions ornamented with gold and silver; many counterpanes and coverlids of beds lined with Ermine; in short, all the walls of the Palace shine with gold and silver. Here is, besides, a certain cabinet called *Paradise*, where besides that everything glitters so with silver, gold, and jewels, as to dazzle one's eyes, there is a musical instrument made all of glass except the strings. Afterwards we were led into the Gardens, which are most pleasant; here we saw rosemary so

---

* Here are several mistakes.

planted and nailed to the walls that it covered them entirely, which is a method exceeding common in *England*.

KINGSTON, a Market Town.

NONESUCH, a royal retreat, in a place formerly called *Cuddington*, a very healthful situation, chosen by King *Henry VIII.* for his pleasure and retirement, and built by him with an excess of magnificence and elegance, even to ostentation; one would imagine everything that architecture could perform to have been employed in this work; there are everywhere so many statues that seem to breathe; so many miracles of consummate art, so many casts that rival even the perfection of *Roman* antiquity, that it may well claim and justify its name of *Nonesuch*, being without an equal, or as the poet sung :

> This which no equal has in Art or Fame,
> Britons deservedly do *Nonesuch* name.

The Palace itself is so encompassed with Parks full of deer, delicious Gardens, Groves ornamented with trellis work, cabinets of verdure, and Walks so embowered by trees, that it seems to be a place pitched upon by *Pleasure* herself to dwell in along with *Health*.

In the pleasure and artificial Gardens are many Columns and Pyramids of Marble, two Fountains that spout water one round the other like a pyramid, upon which are perched small birds that stream water out of their bills. In the Grove of *Diana* is a very agreeable Fountain, which *Actæon* turned into a Stag, as he was sprinkled by the Goddess and her Nymphs, with Inscriptions.

There is besides another Pyramid of marble full of concealed pipes, which spirt upon all who come within their reach.

Returned from thence to *London*.

We set out from *London* in a boat, and fell down the river, leaving GREENWICH, which we have spoken of before, on our right hand.

BARKING, a Town in sight on the left.

GRAVESEND, a small Town, famous for the convenience of its port; the largest *Dutch* ships usually call here. As we were to proceed farther from hence by water, we took our last leave here of the noble *Bohemian, David Strziela,* and his tutor *Tobias Salandar,* our constant fellow-travellers through *France* and *England,* they designing to return home through *Holland,* we on a second tour into *France;* but it pleased Heaven to put a stop to their design, for the worthy *Strziela* was seized with a diarrhœa a few days before our departure, and as we afterwards learned by letters from *Salandar,* died in a few days of a violent fever in *London.*

QUEENBOROUGH, we left the Castle on our right; a little farther we saw them fishing oysters out of the sea, which are nowhere in greater plenty or perfection; witness *Ortelius* in his epitome, etc.

WHITSTABLE, here we went ashore.

CANTERBURY, we came to it on foot; this is the seat of the Archbishop, Primate of all *England,* a very ancient town, and without doubt of note in the time of the *Romans.*

Here are two Monasteries almost contiguous, namely of *Christ* and *St. Augustine,* both of them once filled with Benedictine Monks; the former was afterwards dedicated to *St. Thomas Becket,* the name of Christ being obliterated; it stands almost in the middle of the Town, and with so much majesty lifts itself and its two Towers to a stupendous height, that as *Erasmus* says, it strikes even those who only see it at a distance with awe. In the Choir, which is shut up with iron rails, are the following Monuments :—

King *Henry IV.,* with his Wife *Joan* of *Navarre,* of white marble.

Nicholas Wooton, Privy Counsellor to *Henry VIII.*

Edward VI., Mary and *Elizabeth,* Kings and Queens of *England.*

Of Prince *Edward,* Duke of *Aquitain* and *Cornwall,* and Earl of *Chester.*

Reginald Pole, with this Inscription :—

 The Remains of *Reginald Pole,* Cardinal and Archbishop
     of *Canterbury.*

Cardinal *Chatillon.*

We were then shown the Chair in which the Bishops are placed, when they are installed. In the Vestibule of the Church, on the south side, stands the Statues of three men armed, cut in stone, who slew *Thomas Becket*, Archbishop of Canterbury, made a Saint for his Martyrdom ; their names are adjoined,—

𝔗usci. 𝔍usci. 𝔅erri.*

Being tired with walking, we refreshed ourselves here with a mouthful of bread, and some ale, and immediately mounted post horses, and arrived about two or three o'clock in the morning at DOVER. In our way to it, which was rough and dangerous enough, the following accident happened to us : our Guide or Postillion, a youth, was before with two of our Company, about the distance of a musket shot; we by not following quick enough, had lost sight of our friends ; we came afterwards to where the road divided ; on the right it was down hill and marshy, on the left was a small hill. Whilst we stopped here in doubt, and consulted which of the roads we should take, we saw all on a sudden on our right hand some horsemen, their stature, dress, and horses, exactly resembling those of our friends. Glad of having found them again, we determined to set on after them ; but it happened through God's mercy, that though we called to them, they did not answer us, but kept on down the marshy road, at such a rate, that their horses feet struck fire at every stretch ; which made us with reason begin to suspect that they were thieves, having had warning of such ; or rather that they were nocturnal spectres, who, as we were afterwards told, are frequently seen in those places. There were likewise a great many *Jack W'alanthorns*, so that we were quite seized with horror and amazement! But, fortunately for us, our Guide soon after sounded his horn, and we

---

* This is another most inaccurate account. The murderers of *Becket* were Tracy, Morville, Britton, and Fitzurse.

following the noise, turned down the left hand road, and arrived safe to our companions, who, when we had asked them, if they had not seen the horsemen who had gone by us? Answered, not a soul. Our opinions according to custom were various on this matter ; but whatever the thing was, we were without doubt in imminent danger, for which we escaped, the glory is to be ascribed to God alone.

DOVER, situated among Cliffs (standing where the Port itself was originally, as may be gathered from Anchors, and parts of Vessels dug up there), is famous more for the convenience of its Port, which indeed is now much decayed, and its passage to *France*, than for either its elegance, or populousness. This passage the most used, and the shortest, is of thirty miles, which, with a favourable wind, may be run over in five or six hours time, as we ourselves experienced; some reckon it only eighteen miles to *Calais*, and to *Boulogne* sixteen *English* miles, which, as *Ortelius* says in his *Theatrum*, are longer than the *Italian*.

Here was a Church dedicated to *St. Martin*, by *Victred*, King of *Kent*, and a House belonging to the Knights Templars ; of either there are now no remains. It is the seat of a Suffragan to the Archbishop of *Canterbury*, who, when the Archbishop is employed on business of more consequence, manages the ordinary affairs, but does not interfere with the Archiepiscopal jurisdiction. Upon a hill, or rather rock, which, on its right side, is almost everywhere a precipice, a very extensive Castle rises to a surprising height, in size like a little City, extremely well fortified, and thick set with Towers, and seems to threaten the sea beneath. *Matthew Paris* calls it, the door and key of *England*. The ordinary people have taken it into their heads that it was built by *Julius Caesar*, it is likely it might by the *Romans*, from those *British* bricks in the Chapel, which they made use of in their foundations.—*See Camden's Britannia.*

After we had dined, we took leave of ENGLAND.

75

𝔄 𝔖𝔥𝔬𝔯𝔱 𝔇𝔢𝔰𝔠𝔯𝔦𝔭𝔱𝔦𝔬𝔫 𝔬𝔣 𝔈𝔫𝔤𝔩𝔞𝔫𝔡.

BRITAIN, consisting of the two kingdoms of *England* and *Scotland,* is the largest Island in the World, encompassed by the Ocean, the *German* and *French* Seas. The largest and southern portion of it is *England,* so named from the *Angli,* who quitted the little territory still called *Angel* in the Kingdom of *Denmark,* took possession here. It is governed by its own King, who owns no superior but God. It is divided into 39 Counties, to which 13 in Wales were added by Henry VIII., the first who distributed that principality into Counties; over each of these in times of danger a Lord Lieutenant nominated by the King, presides with an unlimited power. Every year some gentleman, an inhabitant of the place, is appointed Sheriff; his office is to collect the public monies, to raise fines, or to make seizures, and to account for it to the Treasury, to attend upon the Judges, and put their sentence in execution, to empannel the Jury who sit upon facts, and return their verdict to the Judges (who in *England* are only such of the law, and not of the fact), to convey the condemned to execution, and to determine in lesser causes, for the greater are tried by the Judges, formerly called Travelling Judges, now Judges of Assize; these go their Circuits through the counties twice every year to hear causes, and pronounce sentence upon prisoners.

As to Ecclesiastical Jurisdiction, after the Popes had assigned a Church and a Parish to every Priest, *Honorius,* Archbishop of *Canterbury,* about the year 636, began to divide England in the same manner into Parishes. As it has two provinces, so it has two Archbishops, the one of *Canterbury,* Primate and Metropolitan of All *England,* the other of *York;* subject to these are 25 Bishops, viz.: 22 to *Canterbury,* and the remaining three to *York.*

The soil is fruitful, and abounds with cattle, which inclines the inhabitants rather to feeding than ploughing, so that near a third of the land is left uncultivated for grazing. The climate is most temperate at all times, and the air never heavy, consequently maladies are scarcer, and less Physic is used there than anywhere else. There are but few Rivers. Though the Soil is productive it bears no wine,

76

but that want is supplied from abroad by the best kinds, as of *Orleans, Gascon, Rhenish*, and *Spanish*.

The general drink is beer, which is prepared from barley, and is exceedingly well tasted, but strong, and what soon fuddles. There are many hills without one tree or any springs, which produce a very short and tender grass, and supply plenty of food to sheep. Upon these wander numerous flocks, extremely white, and whether from the temperature of the air, or goodness of the earth, bearing softer and finer fleeces than those of any other country. This is the true Golden Fleece, in which consist the chief riches of the inhabitants, great sums of money being brought into the country by merchants, chiefly for that article of trade. The dogs here are particularly good. It has Mines of Gold, Silver, and Tin (of which all manner of table utensils are made, in brightness equal to silver and used all over *Europe*), of Lead, and of Iron, but not much of the latter. The horses are small but swift. Glass Houses are in plenty here.

Of the Manners of the English.

The *English* are serious like the *Germans*, lovers of Show, liking to be followed wherever they go by whole troops of servants, who wear their masters arms in silver, fastened to their left arms, a ridicule they deservedly lay under. They excel in dancing and music. They are active and lively, though of a thicker make than the *French*; they cut their hair close on the middle of the head, letting it grow on either side; they are good Sailors and better Pirates, cunning, treacherous, and thievish; above 300 are said to be hanged annually in *London;* beheading with them is less infamous than hanging. They give the wall as the place of honour. Hawking is the general sport of the gentry. They are more polite in eating than the *French*, devouring less bread, but more meat, which they roast in perfection. They put a great deal of sugar in their drink. Their Beds are covered with Tapestry, even those of Farmers. They are often molested with the Scurvy, said to have first crept into *England* with the *Norman* Conquest. Their houses are commonly of two stories, except in *London*, where they are of three and four, though but seldom of four; they are built of wood, those of the richer sort with bricks; their roofs are low, and where the owner has money, covered with Lead.

They are powerful in the field, successful against their enemies, impatient of anything like slavery, vastly fond of great noises that fill the ear, such as the firing of cannons, drums, and the ringing of bells, so that it is common for a number of them, that have a glass in their heads, to go up into some belfrey and ring the bells for hours together for the sake of exercise. If they see a Foreigner, very well made or particularly handsome, they will say, " *It is a pity he is not an Englishman.*"

𝔗𝔥𝔢 𝔍𝔩𝔩𝔲𝔰𝔱𝔯𝔦𝔬𝔲𝔰 𝔉𝔞𝔪𝔦𝔩𝔦𝔢𝔰 𝔬𝔣 𝔈𝔫𝔤𝔩𝔞𝔫𝔡.

THOMAS HOWARD.—Duke of Norfolk, hereditary Marshal of England; the Dutchy is extinct for rebellion, the last Duke being beheaded.

GREY.—Duke of Suffolk, attainted under Queen Mary.

PHILIP HOWARD.—Earl of Arundel, in his mother's right, and of Surrey by his father, son of the above mentioned Duke of Norfolk, he himself condemned for high Treason, and his titles forfeited.

EDWARD VERE.—Earl of Oxford, hereditary Chamberlain of England.

PERCY.—Earl of Northumberland, descended from the Dukes of Brabant.

CHARLES NEVILL.—Earl of Westmoreland, banished into Holland, and deprived of his fortune and dignities for rebellion.

TALBOT.—Earl of Shrewsbury.

GREY.—Earl of Kent, has but a small Estate.

STANLEY.—Earl of Derby. King of Man.

MANNERS.—Earl of Rutland.

SOMERSET.—Earl of Worcester, descended from a bastard of the Somerset Family, which itself is of the royal Family of the Plantagenets.

CLIFFORD.—Earl of Cumberland.

RATCLIFF.—Earl of Sussex.

HASTINGS.—Earl of Huntingdon, of the line of York, by the mother's side.

BOURCHIER.—Earl of Bath.

78

AMBROSE SUTTON *alias* DUDLEY.—Earl of Warwick, died a few years since childless.

WRIOTHESLY.—Earl of Southampton.

RUSSEL.—Earl of Bedford.

HERBERT.—Earl of Pembroke.

EDWARD SEYMOUR.—Earl of Herford, son of the Duke of Somerset, who was beheaded in the reign of Edward VI.

ROBERT SUTTON or DUDLEY.—Earl of Leicester, brother of the Earl of Warwick, died a few years ago.

ROBERT D'EVREUX.—Earl of Essex, and Ewe in Normandy, created hereditary Marshal of England in 1598.

CHARLES HOWARD.—Of the Norfolk family, created Earl of Nottingham 1597, Lord High Admiral of England, and Privy Counsellor.

FIESNES.—Earl of Lincoln.

BROWN.—Viscount Montacute.

HOWARD.—Of the Norfolk family, Viscount Bindon.

NEVIL.—Baron Abergavenny; this Barony is controverted.

TOUCHET.—Baron Audley.

ZOUCH.—Baron Zouch.

PEREGRIN BERTIE.—Baron Willoughby of Eresby and Brooke, Governor of Berwick.

BERKLEY.—Baron Berkley, of the antient family of the Kings of Denmark.

PARKER.—Baron Morley.

DACRE.—Baron Dacre of Gyllesland, this Barony is vacant.

DACRE.—Baron Dacre of the South, he died four years since, and the Barony devolved on his daughter.

BROOKE.—Baron Cobham, Warden of the Cinque Ports.

STAFFORD.—Baron Stafford, reduced to want, he is heir to the family of the Duke of Buckingham, who were hereditary Constables of England.

GRAY.—Baron Gray of Wilton.

SCROOP.—Baron Scroop of Boulton.

SUTTON.—Baron Dudley.

STOURTON.—Baron Stourton.

NEVILL.—Baron Latimer, died some years since, without heirs male, the title controverted.

LUMLEY.—Baron Lumley. 79

BLUNT.—Baron Mountjoy.

OGLE.—Baron Ogle.

DARCY.—Baron Darcy.

PARKER.—Baron Montegle, son and heir of Baron Morley, he has his Barony in right of his mother, of the family of Stanley.

SANDYS.—Baron Sandys.

VAUX.—Baron Vaux.

WINDSOR.—Baron Windsor.

WENTWORTH.—Baron Wentworth.

BOROUGH.—Baron Borough, reduced to want.

Baron MORDAUNT.

Baron EURE.

Baron RICH.

Baron SHEFFIELD.

Baron NORTH, Privy Counsellor, and Treasurer of the Household.

Baron HUNSDON, Privy Counsellor and Lord Chamberlain.

SACKVILLE.—Baron Buckhurst, Privy Counsellor.

CECIL, Thomas.—Baron Burleigh, son of the Treasurer, yet a child; he holds the Barony in right of his mother, daughter of the Earl of Rutland.

HOWARD of Maltravers, son of the Earl of Arundel, not yet restored in blood.

Baron CHENY.

Baron CROMWELL.

Baron WHARTON.

Baron WILLOUGHBY of Parham.

Baron PAGETT, in exile, attainted.

Baron CHANDOIS.

Baron ST JOHN.

Baron DELEWARE, his ancestors took the King of France prisoner.

Baron COMPTON, has squandered almost all his substance.

Baron NORRIS.

HOWARD, Thomas, second son of the Duke of Norfolk, Baron Audley of Saffron Walden, in his mother's right.

HOWARD, William, third son of the Duke of Norfolk, is neither a Baron, nor yet restored in blood.

The End.

www.ingramcontent.com/pod-product-compliance
Lightning Source LLC
Chambersburg PA
CBHW031756090426
42739CB00008B/1031